Stephen Curry

The Best

DAVE JACKSON

Introduction

Stephen Curry is a professional basketball player, and many people think he is one of the best basketball players in history. Stephen is definitely one of the best shooters ever, and he has won a lot of awards.

Stephen Curry's dad also played professional basketball in the National Basketball Association, which is usually called the NBA. So, Stephen had a little help from his dad in learning how to play basketball, but Stephen is a professional because he was patient and he worked hard, not just because of his dad.

Early Life

Stephen Curry grew up around professional basketball players and coaches. His dad, Dell Curry, played for the NBA team the Charlotte Hornets. Charlotte is a city in North Carolina, and Stephen grew up there. Stephen's dad played for the Hornets for most of his career. But he also played for a few other teams too. This means that Stephen and his brother and sister got to travel a lot.

But Stephen's mom and dad also made sure they always did their school work. Stephen's mom actually worked at the school that Stephen and his siblings went to, so there was no chance they could skip out on doing their homework!

His dad took Stephen to games where he was sometimes allowed to shoot baskets with the team. Being on the basketball court in front of thousands of people must have been amazing! So, from a very young age, Stephen was able to play basketball and get tips from professionals. But he also got plenty of tips from his school coaches, too.

Stephen started playing and watching basketball when he was really young. He worked hard and practiced, and when he was in middle school, he was playing for the school team. His dad had been traded to the NBA team in Toronto, Canada. While he was in middle school in Toronto, his basketball team had an undefeated season, which means they didn't lose a single game!

High School

By the time Stephen went to high school, his family was living back in Charlotte, North Carolina. The families of professional athletes sometimes have to move a lot because the athletes can change which team they play for. But Stephen's dad retired from playing when Stephen was fourteen. And since his dad had played in Charlotte for ten years, the family moved back there.

While Stephen was in high school, he played basketball, too. His first year of high school, Stephen was only five feet, four inches tall. Most professional basketball players are more than six feet tall, and some of them are even seven feet tall!

A basketball hoop is ten feet off the ground, so a seven foot tall player could stand on the ground and reach up and touch the hoop without even jumping! But when Stephen stood on the ground during his first year of high school, his head was just barely half way as tall as the hoop.

But as he got older, he got quite a bit taller. By the time he graduated from high school, he was six feet tall. He wouldn't be able to touch the hoop without jumping, but that didn't matter because he was so good at all the other parts of basketball.

In high school, Stephen practiced and practiced and practiced. He played high school basketball in the winter, and played in youth basketball leagues when the school wasn't playing. He worked hard, stayed in shape, ate healthy, and listened to his parents and coaches.

Because he did all that, Stephen got to be really good at basketball. Really, really good. His team went to the playoffs for the whole state three times! And not only was the team awesome, Stephen won all sorts of awards too. He was an all star, and a lot of college coaches would come to watch Stephen and his team practice.

College

Stephen wanted to play basketball in college more than anything. All through high school he kept good grades while practicing basketball all the time too. But for some reason, even though he had good grades and was great at basketball and was a nice and friendly person, not too many colleges offered him scholarships, which is where the college pays for all or most of the cost of college.

Stephen did get offered a scholarship to a few colleges. He decided to go to a college that hadn't won a big basketball game in almost thirty years! That would change because Stephen had become a crazy good shooter. He could make baskets from pretty much anywhere on the basketball court!

He was especially good at making three point shots, which are the hardest shots to make. You usually get only two points for making a basket, but there is a line on the court that marks where you can make three point shots.

The line goes in an arch around almost half the court, and you have to be standing behind the line to get three points. Stephen was one of the best at making these three point shots. In his first year of college, Stephen set the record for most three point shots made by a freshman! He also set the record for his college for scoring more points than any other freshman who had ever played basketball at that college.

And then the very next year, he set the record for most three pointers made by any player in college ever! He set another record that year too. This one for scoring the most points during the season. Stephen was starting to be known as one of the best basketball shooters in the whole country, and the NBA teams were really paying attention to him.

Remember how the college he went to hadn't won a playoff game in a really long time? Well, that changed when Stephen started playing there. With Stephen making so many three pointers and scoring so many points, the team was bound to win more games. They even went to the biggest college basketball tournament in the entire United States, and they won a whole bunch of games! Stephen's team even beat one of the best teams in the country.

Even though college is usually four years long, Stephen decided that he should start playing professional basketball without graduating first. A lot of college athletes do this because professional athletes make a lot of money. So they sometimes leave college early so that can start making money. But Stephen said that he would continue to work on getting his college degree, he just wasn't going to go to college full time.

National Basketball Association

After deciding that he was not going to finish his fourth year of college, Stephen entered what is called the NBA Draft. The draft is where all the NBA teams get to choose which new players they would like to have on their team.

The draft is made up of mostly college kids, but there may be a few who graduated high school, but didn't go to college. The way the draft works is that the team with the worst record gets to choose first. Usually the team who won the championship the year before chooses last. It's kind of like picking sides in a pick-up baseball game.

Stephen was picked (drafted) by a California team called the
Golden State Warriors. He was picked as the seventh pick, which

is really good! There are hundreds of guys in the draft who are trying to be professional basketball players, so being picked in the top ten is pretty amazing.

In his first year playing professional basketball, Stephen almost won another important award. Writers who write about basketball are asked who they think the best rookie is. Stephen came in second in the voting for Rookie of the Year, which is still a really great honor. He was also selected for the All-Star team made up of other rookies (a rookie is someone who is playing their first year).

But during his rookie year, Stephen was just getting warmed up. In his second year playing professional basketball, Stephen won the Sportsman of the Year award, which is for people who are nice to others and play within the rules.

He also set another record, just like he always was. Basketball players take a lot of shots, but they don't make every single one. For example, if you take ten shots and make five of them, you scored fifty percent of the time. If you took ten shots and made nine of them, then you're scoring ninety percent of the time, which is amazing. Stephen scored on more than ninety three percent of his shots, which was a team record. He basically never missed!

During his third year of playing professionally, Stephen was hurt a lot, and didn't get to play much. He had to have surgery on his ankle, and then hurt the same ankle again just after being able to start playing again. Professional athletes often get hurt, but because they are so strong and in shape, they can sometimes come back pretty quickly. But sometimes, the injury just gets worse, and the only way to make it better is to take some time off.

This is what Stephen did, and he was back in top playing shape for his fourth year. Once again, he was breaking records left and right. He broke the team record for most three pointers scored in a game. And Stephen broke the whole NBA record for scoring more three pointers over the season than anyone else in history.

This was also the first year that Stephen went to the NBA playoffs. Even though the team played well and won the first round of games, they lost before they could get to the championship.

In Stephen's fourth year of playing, his team again went to the playoffs, and Stephen broke another record. He broke the team record for most three pointers made by any one person. At that point he had scored seven hundred and one to break the record, but this was early in his career, and he has been adding to that total for a few more years now.

Stephen was also selected to the NBA All Star team, for the second time. Players get elected to the team by NBA fans voting on who they think the best players in the league are.

The fifth year he played saw Stephen break more records, and again get voted onto the All Star team. In fact, he broke his own record by making two hundred and seventy three three pointers. This was one more three pointer than he had made a couple of years before.

He also became the fastest player in NBA history to score one thousand three pointers. He's not the only person to do this, but it took him playing in a lot less games than anyone else to get to that level.

But Stephen's professional career isn't limited to just playing in the NBA. He has also played for Team USA in the Olympics, and has even won two gold medals for playing basketball!

Impact on Basketball

Stephen Curry has been a fantastic basketball player since he started playing. And even though a lot of the bigger colleges looked over him, they are certainly regretting that now. Stephen has become one of the best shooters in the NBA. Some people are even saying that he might be the best shooter in NBA history.

Stephen has had an impact on modern basketball even though he's only been playing professionally for five years. For a long time, there have been truly great basketball players, but none of them could shoot like Stephen. They could make great passes and slam dunks, but not many of them could be so far away from the hoop and still make baskets the way Stephen does.

This means that as more young people like yourself start to play basketball and watch the professionals, more and more kids will try to be really good at three pointers or taking jump shots. Stephen's impact on the NBA is happening right now, but in a few years when kids get older, we will see more and more shooters like Stephen.

But Stephen's legacy isn't just about making three pointers and scoring baskets whenever he wants. He is also a very, very nice person. He has won the Sportsmanship Award, and likes to help out with a lot of charities too. He raises money to help animals, children, and sick people.

This is how he uses his fame for good things. There are tons of people who would like to meet Stephen, and sometimes they can pay money so that they can meet him face to face. Stephen doesn't keep the money they pay, though. He takes that money and donates it to charity.

Future

Stephen is a young guy, and will probably be able to play in the NBA for quite a few more years. The average NBA player only plays for six or seven years. Stephen has already played for five years. But the average number of years includes far more people who only played for a year or two. So Stephen should be able to play for at least a couple more years. But he might play another five or ten. Imagine how many records he'll have then!

One of the biggest factors of how long a professional athlete can play is how many injuries they have. Stephen had trouble with his ankle and missed a lot of one season. But, that was the only year he was hurt. All through high school, college, and most of his professional years, Stephen has been healthy. That's good news for those of us who really like to watch him play!

Conclusion

Stephen Curry is young, strong, and healthy. That is part of the reason he is so good. But really, he is so good for other reasons. Stephen practiced hard, and never gave up. Even when he was passed over by colleges, Stephen didn't let that get him down. He simply went to a college he liked, and proved just how wrong the big colleges were in passing him over.

Stephen is the kind of athlete and person we should all try to be. He is friendly and courteous, hard working and dedicated, and uses his skills to entertain millions of people, all while raising money for charities.

Even though he got a bit of a head start in basketball because of his dad, Stephen did not rely on that to get him into the NBA. He relied on the good advice of his parents and coaches so that he could be possibly one of the greatest players in NBA history.

He doesn't set out just to make and break basketball records. Stephen goes out to play the best and hardest he can, even if he doesn't break a record or win every single game. Stephen knows that in all team sports, sometimes the best player is the one who can pass the ball to teammates so they can score.

Stephen Curry had a pretty good childhood, but even if he hadn't, he would still probably be in the NBA. He never gave up, never quit working or studying, and in the end, he has become not only a great basketball player, but also a great person.

From the Author

Thank you very much for downloading and reading this book. I hope that you find the information useful and interesting.

If you enjoyed the book, please take a moment to share your opinion with other on the book page.

Still craving for more interesting basketball books? I recommend you to check out my other books below that are also available for a great price.

KOBE BRYANT
The Legend

DAVE JACKSON

LEBRON JAMES

The Greatest

DAVE JACKSON

KEVIN DURANT
The Star

DAVE JACKSON

Photo Credits

Keith Allison

Copyright

Copyright © 2015 by Dave Jackson.